THE P·E·R·S·O·N·I·F·I·E·D STREET

·

POEMS 1974- 1978

BY

THOMAS RAIN CROWE

WITH AN INTRODUCTION BY JACK HIRSCHMAN

·

New Native Press

Cover print: "Death." Stanislaus Szukalski

Acknowledgement here to the editors of the following periodicals in
which the following poems first appeared: "Fear" in **Amerus #1**.
"No Such Thing As Prose" in **Beatitude #25.** "Sometimes A Piece
of Light" in **Iron**. "The Test" in **Waters #4**. "Petition To The Sun"
in **Beatitude #28**. "I Watch Rats" in **Iron** (special spring issue
1977). "What The Land Sings" in **Waters** (special fall issue 1977:
"The Native Americans"). "Something Dark" in **Beatitude #26**.
"Alliternation" in **Paper Air**. "Wind in A Galleon's Sails" in North
Carolina Poetry Society **Award Winning Poems**, 1980.

Acknowledgement to Atheneum Press for permission to use text from
Selected Poems: Osip Mandelstam (Atheneum, 1974) for the poem
"The Age Is Dying" in this collection.
Credit to New Directions Pub. for use of quote from the poem "City"
from *Illuminations*, by Arthur Rimbaud (*Illuminations*, Arthur
Rimbaud, New Directions, 1957).

FIRST EDITION

Book design by Dana Irwin

A special thanks to Ken Long for his unselfish friendship and
inspiration; and to Darci Farrow, for her gift of a second life....

New Native books and broadsides are published for New Native Press. Book
orders and information should be addressed to: Rt. 67 Box 128, Cullowhee,
N.C. 28723.

Library of Congress Catalog Card # 93-092608

ISBN 1-883197-01-5

To: The Darkness, and those who have gone down...

CONTENTS

III. THE LANGUAGE OF KNIVES

(untitled)
Poetry
Petition To The Sun
Poem To da Vinci Bathing
The Language Of Knives
Memory
Expectation
La Magique Du Bonheur
I Watch Rats
The Association
Sierra Blood
What The Land Sings
Drouth
The Difference
The Muse

IV. THE PERSONIFIED STREET

Something Dark
The Edge
Juliet's Wait
The Personified Street
Noumenon
The Rhythms Of Loss
The Scrubber
Alliternation
In Red Snow
Pretense Is Not War
The Final Oar
The Answer
Of Shroud; Of Sea; Of Me...

INTRODUCTION

I first met Thomas Crowe (the later adopted continental-american name, literally taken from the name Dawson by which he was known to me for four years) on the streets of North Beach, S.F. He asked after my work and I directed him to my most 'painterly' of books, AUR SEA. From there, Tom became, for three years, an important part of what was to become and to be known as the Beatitude cadre: traveling to the Folsom Prison Creative Writers Workshop together, the northcoastal headlands, and in and around the S. F. Bay Area on various literary jaunts and missions; he edited the very important 25th issue of Beatitude magazine---the international texts of which are a credit to both the streets of San Francisco and the motherland of revolution in general; and, perhaps most energetically, it was he who virtually single-handedly sustained the "menial" and organizational homework for the Beatitude-City Lights readings, various social and political rallies and readings such as the Proposition 15 benefit (the California referendum initiative concerning nuclear safeguards), and Beatitude books and magazines, and later the S.F. International Poetry Festival of which he was founder and director-coordinator in 1976. Collusions both personal and poetic drove him away from the street and to the land which his Carolina boyhood continually evoked, but his work for the Beatitude group and for the poetry and socio-political community in northern California certainly is not forgotten.

Tom early reminded me in style of Jim Gill, a texan painter with whom I'd worked in Los Angeles, who likewise, after much city life, took to the northern California land (in Tom's case, more specifically to the Sierra foothills along the North San Juan Ridge) to develop; and his poetry---at times "awkward" blurts of power and protest, at times elusively moving reflections of the soul in the motion of discovery itself---reminded me at first of the very early work of Clayton Eshleman in Indiana. The Russian poets moved him deeply, though his native-american urges "felt" the revolution perhaps more in terms of the French. Like both Gill and Eshleman there is in his work a continual search through "foreign poets," in whose intuitions his poetic psyche is entangled with respect and challenge, for he is a country boy at heart, but aware and involved as well in a sense of international revolution. It is perhaps a sense of the purity of revolution, and the paradoxes therefrom that most define this volume. No doubt his "Betrayal" poem to the Beatitude group indicts the dirty-handedness of street wheeling-dealing in the name of politics, and expresses a bitterness that perhaps only could be resolved by a return to roots in the land; and in "No Such Thing As Prose," a poem dedicated to me, he captures with beautiful negative accuracy many of my own intuitions and hopes. I say negative because as in other poems in this volume there is a sense of a man in a world of poetry searching for a certain virtuistic paradigm, a dialectic whose intuition has seized him in a way he can define only by his despair. Thus when he writes: "There is little truth in what is false/And no such thing as prose" he is uttering the words both in "dogmatic" strength and despair, for dogma, alone, is never really strong. But what underlies the paradox is Crowe's quest for a literal Truth---even apparently outside of the passion of the lone image; and this links his work with many and much that are in line with the tradition of Transformation, in quest of the meaning and pursuit of spiritual Work (such as poetry itself) in a society as hard-edged as ours.

When he writes:

"I AM THE TWENTIETH CENTURY!

and have the right
to live or die."

he is uttering a very simple yet very profound cry of despair against the necessity of decay which has been realized as the ideology of capitalist America.

It is in such cries, as they emerge from Indian depths through exploitations which poets like Mayakovsky and Esenin renounced, which are the meat of the anguish of Crowe's poetry, and which will, in books to come, and as he understands more richly the red earth that sustains his songs, resonate with even greater impact. For he has chosen many "maitres" to align his receptions to. And they are---as he has called them out---going to nourish his future expressions, along with the "they" that often is given political or even sexual connotation in this book but who are, in fact, the gateway to the understanding of that ideology which is the poetry of evolution and of true communism itself.

Jack Hirschman
August 1978

PREFACE

Not wanting to hide behind the mask of literary anonymity, neither that of literary fame; these, then, are poems in testament of the exploration of practically every corner and aspect of the "American Dream"---and a book in homage to my teachers---written from road and land's end in S.F. from early 1974 and my somewhat less than "grande" entrance through her golden gates, until 1977, where I served literary apprenticeship to the traditions and older writers who still inhabit her memories, streets, and cafes. The personified street. A life of feelings personified through the directly-encountered realities of the "rue noir" ... looking back into the eyes of the american night, and almost anachronistically reflecting my thoughts born in younger years, only now emerging mature in the face of darkness, in the face of the monster itself: the shroud-storied highrise walls of scientific single-vision and the supra-intellectual rationality of the 20th century.... These pages came as a result of my love for San Francisco in particular, and my disgust for cities and the urban mentality in general. Therefore, it is a situation of paradox reality from which I wrote these words. As I was, and as Nietzsche says, not more than "a fly in the marketplace, where men only seek to befriend you in hate, and to suck your blood." Where "the people have little idea of greatness, that is to say, creativeness. But they have a taste for all presenters and actions of great things---" so then these poems represent, foremost, a reaction. And I believe that they are valid in that sense. The fact that I no longer believe in the creative validity of reactionism in my own life's search does not lighten or change the feeling nature of these phrases, or invalidate their cause. For at the time, their cause (that of a concerned rEvolutionary) was cause enough to inspire their delivery onto the page. And in terms of "text," it represented truth and struggle as I knew it then. Validity in the Emersonian sense that "only that soul can be my friend which I encounter on the line of my own march, that soul to which I do not decline, and which does not decline to me, but, native of the same celestial latitude, repeats in its own way all my experience." It is to such a soul that these words go out. That they for some other may represent, in comfort, their own experiences; or in vision, their own dreams. I can only say in this regard, that my ideological sentiments take on an even greater Emersonian posture in light of his statement: "Not in reaction but in action do---." And by way of the idea that men may only teach by doing. And further, that "all men plume themselves on the improvement of society, and no man improves."

This book, then, is a reflection of a period of growth in my life. Nothing more. And nothing less. A cumulation of consciousness over a quarter century. The written rites-of-passage into american manhood. An extension of the continuing struggle for merger of body with mind, and beyond. The search into the collective unconscious for the source of that connection. The primordial search for the root of paradox! These words and images merely express what I have seen of myself, and others, through these eyes. Inside, find growing pains. The darkness. Visions of horror, frustration, and disappointment of the things I have witnessed, and the planes I have traveled, through that life. Also, the ecstatic presence of an occasional glimpse, miragistically, of love, hope, and dreams realized. What I have lived and grown through. The shields and masks of arrogance I have, now, found little or no need of and have thrown aside. Always chipping away, psycho-archeologically, at my outer shell. Tearing at the mask. To become more <u>vulnerable</u>. Finding and giving strength to that <u>inside myself</u>. Seeking <u>inner strength</u>, and the legs that let me dance! There is little of this here, however; for that is the period I have entered only now, writing back across the desert of these old words. That is another mirror. Another book. Another life, that I am only beginning to experience and share with friends, Nature, and those persons, those ideas, which I love.

In a time when language and all aspects of the historical are in need of (and are going through an unprecedented) change; I no longer know the words of these pages. They are friends who have disappeared, but who were an important part of the reasons for why I am who I am now, with the ability to look back; AND OFTEN SMILE. For there is no future in a frown. Making an ally of love. A partner of hope. A companion of pain...

There is a spill of passion and anger in this work which parallels my continuous reach toward strength (survival) through tenderness, sensitivity, surrender, and faith. When the lake is full, the gates of the dam(n) must be opened to let the excess drain. Living within a system of corporate imperialistic religiosity in the West, there is often an excess of dehumanized anger and passion. In truth, the gates are often lifted. The body rarely sleeps.

T.R.C.

San Francisco 11/77

"Beholding from afar I saw a great cloud looming black over all the earth, that had absorbed the earth which covered my soul."

-Thomas Aquinas

I. FEAR

The artist makes a butterfly,
puts rainbow dust on her wings, and places
her on a sunflower---tender---silently....
---Then! the sweat and blood-soaked hand
of a pork-packer reaches for the butterfly,
and to make it useful, he crushes it and
gives it to the ducks for food....
---This is Democracy!

-Stanislaus   Szukalski

THE SYSTEM

To get what they wanted
they used me.
To do what I wanted to do
I used them.
To see what they wanted to see
they used us all.
To be what we wanted to be

it did not exist.

CAPITAL

It was pompous to ask

"Who is matron here?"

Walking in under disappointment's wings
rain dripping from hair
like dogs after a long spring

They seemed like love with an ass's head
through eyes
even the eyes of marble could not feel
Something gray
Something like a stranger's mask
before he takes your life

I walked through the meeting as if
the sky weren't there
toward a sign on a backroom door
saying:
              "Private
                  Police"

They were playing games with
people they had
lined up in rows
Green bills
heaped-up in piles on the board
over which they all leaned
through the smoke of excess and blame

What I had
they did not want

What I wanted
they could not conceive

MEDIA

for Thomas Edison

If there's a blade at my throat
I'll give in to what you want
But if there are stars in the sky tonight
you lose---

In those rooms of blue death
and white lies:
Minds like old shoes handed down
through families of poor
Pictures of Earth
taken from a spendthrift moon
Long trains
running on tracks of violent ink---

What love was
was a wish to believe
Beauty like Christmas wrapping sleep

They have metamorphized the dream
into math
or vespers at the shrine of a watch
Where lawyers and seedy priests write poems
through neon and plastic straws

And if they have lowered the rent from the sky
I'll move into my own Space
like a laughing dog at the breath of a cat he can't see
Where pain is the price of a young girl
And the women in gardens talking Bosch
to spring and the styrofoam air
Is how they have converted hands
to religious dough
As threes are becoming a pair

OPIUM

after Cocteau

To take one step ahead of Hell
or the day to come
with nothing in mind
came the dawn

Time that snakes saw
crawl
slither through
the silver gates of sex
Where mermaids stood
tall on dry land
And a sousaphone sang
the tunes of a desert sphinx
to the deafened ears of rhyme
beating black drums...

Go on! you to and fro of knives
You electric lines of Nijinsky's night
All you boy scouts of the bourgeoisie!

I have seen the feet of victory dance
in a piano's dream
walking on the microphone neck of chance
Opium in the lung of livingrooms
Water in the veins of brick

Dope-doctors won't reveal
the answers to "the question of faith"
White books
won't gather and display our rust
And what is this ship that sails silk
near the ivory coast of France?
The wish that s's rhyme?
A prayer for bells
on the scales of a famous crop?

No more!
Or less than what we've earned

Not a penny in the eyes of claim
Not a red cent
in the pockets of upper class

IT'S DEAD

Dull is dull on all sides
Like green is usually green
to the sky
When lonely wind
is making love to idealist rain
"A morphine addict's blood shows no trace of morphine"
And choice is addicted to pain

GUNS

"Shoot," she said.
And the orders were to kill.
Anything that moved.
A gust of wind
didn't stand a chance against
the aim of those guns---

That night
as Earth in the way of the Sun
cut off corners of the Moon,
a country died
from time in a line with their sleep.
And the guns stood watch.
Standing guard over
cows down on one knee.
With narrow frowning eyes
searched the darkness for
the faintest sign of light...

In those days
we got up
and went to bed in rows.
Whispered love in
only the safest place.
And grew old.

Is there anything unknown?
Pity that only branches take to trees.
A shame
that the only things that weep
are eyes.
I want to see a cloud that can dance
in the streets of a bullet's pain.
And a tear on the cheeks of law.

A barrel of death is
only equal to one good piece of dirt.
A trigger of me or mine only
fast as someone's tongue.
Good god how I've listened to their prayers!
Steel against the spine of my dreams.
"Join," they'd say.
But I'll be damned if I'll
wear that metal badge a brain!

RECITAL

They wanted me to dance
or shake till they felt full of fear

I was walking on feet
sore from stone roads
and the illusion of someone to love
in meadows
or there in green fields...

For the sound of applause
I was to cut my wrists with joy
and the sharp blade
of nights alone
in the cities of heaven come hell

They took it all

They took it back home in brown bags
for the dogs
and their young that had fallen asleep
And they wrote the next day
in the lines they had paid for with God:

"We paid to see him dance!"

And blood ran from the wounds
between the small and large toes...

Alone with the velvet and wood.

Light that shines through
small odd holes in a door
To eyes that are drowned in the words
of a thousand years of sand

FEAR

If it threatens
then it is not alone
If it sings
then we know that it's in pain

A purple pansy grows
at the foot of every tree
like a proud man
never weeps
And for all the fuss
we've painted red shoes
the colour of dust
we carry around in our veins
If it threatens
then it is not alone
It is making love to
a sexless clock
Or pulling string
from empty boots

They asked me from where
the wind blew
And I said "east"
Like the north
from where I had been
and couldn't go back

TOO MANY CARS IN MY BLOOD

and not enough rice for their starving eyes
Where firebombs
are still playing tag with their dreams
Or poets put in lines
to be shot
or shot-up with
or the "strain"
or the right to bear young
on their own arms--

This time I say "no"
In the face of any fear
I'll say "no" again
Or a third time
"No!"
Until no one's face is white
And fear cries
Or whimpers away like a coward dog
to die
Like a million men that were free
And the women in their eyes

BETRAYAL

to the Beatitude...

So sad
the switch
buddyfuck
and the sway
or the bitch of threes
through fame
and the need to be famous
rich
and alone in your own bed...

We say goodbye
like a candle dies
out of wax
and everything goes black
and everything is white
like clean towels
before the fight
and one in the corner
blue---

War to the tug of
dry tunes
on a piano of lies
or mirrors painted in the colours
we want to see through
and are reflected in
hurt too much to be real---

Farewell all kin
when we were weaned
on a notion of change
and now to the dumps
and to dickens with
love in a cause that was pure
as pure red
as white as our city skin
as blue as the rooms of tv

as yellow as the streak that
runs our backs
turned on the truth we found in poems

HYMN TO OTERO

*"...everything looks dark now, but I saw
and I kept faith."*

from "Fidelity"
-Blas de Otero

I carry the teeth of night
in the pocket of my winter coat.
Down roads where no one sees.
And nothing lasts.

As a boy I watched trains
and drank rain
straight from the sky.
The metal gate closes.
Schools that are zoos for the mind
and the rich.
In their own right
they're still only young.
And I will think again
before I say yes to something
my body feels a lie.

We look sad in lines
at the door of the moon.
I think we'll all be
manservants
and midwives
to what it costs to be free.
The sun stands stern at the gate,
whip in hand.

My country far behind.

Nowhere to go.

MANNERS IN THE EYE OF AN OLD CLOCK

*"But one thing is clear---that the
man who is not 'irritable' is no poet."*

-Edgar Allen Poe

As early as five I am listening to Bach
Bombs in the black brain of
red sleep
Or the way words divide
into numbers in even rows

She drove pins into the base of my neck
Poured lead hot into the heels
of the shoes that let me dance

And I forgave

Like a good saint
Or manners in the eye of an old clock
The tide has turned and
now there's more salt than sea

To make the abstract real
we rolled grenades
into the aisles of every film
It seems my left foot
is always asking my right eye
for the directions to space
And I've stood on the same Earth
for years
For years they'll mix hairspray
in their drinks
Collect whistles and canes...

In the eyes of The Great Aesthete
the fashion of war
looks no more sheik than
an elk in an expensive robe

It's clear

We are children of war
Babes of the guts of machine
Like the thick frozen ice
is keeping our bodies
away from what we believe...

Behind the mask
there is more air
and maybe more light
than in any country town
Prudence weeping rubies
through eyes of the cosmic blush

Rome on the pedals of a fugue

The village rich

NO SUCH THING AS PROSE

"Every public has the Shakespeare it deserves."

-Andre Gide

for Jack Hirschman

Shave my beard old whore
and I'll sing
Even go to old stone huts and pray
to a wooden cross
stuck up in a loft
like a nest that everyone can see
While winter birds turn red
and I wash my time alone in your
ivory skin

There were boys that would come to her
and beg
How she tied them to their dreams
How they nursed her perfect breasts
Fed on the lightning in her veins
She waves with both hands and
they're gone...

The silver eye of the street
has shut with sleep
So who has wings for sale?
And where are they storing up myth
like wet hay in a small mow?
To be pensive in an age of idleness
does as much good
as trying to row a tin boat up the face
of a grandfather clock
When I have been sentenced to a life
I clutch like a gun

I have signed a contract with Deutsche Grammophon
to record the sounds of pain
my body feels each time I fall in love
Outside
there are Nazis in the rain
Women with blue beards
and red rings around their store-bought eyes
Everyone's hating the sleet
and building fires
There is little truth in what is false
And no such thing as prose

THE MARRIAGE OF MACHINE
AND THE 4th DIMENSION

Tonight the world weeps
A great holiday has taken the globe by surprise
This is marriage of machine and the fourth dimension
Somnolence sitting on the steps of hell
Holy Roman eyes
glowing like embers burn through priceless cloth
Even the handsaws have lost their nerve
As a crazed mankind is holding his picnics in a storm
and his rainbows in a zoo

"Do you take this earth?"
In sickness it's the same as in health
Life is a quack!
Every pass of the knife
a danger to the brain---

The ancients are amongst us
They carry torches through the streets of our surprise
They are driving nails
into the wood of our words that are free
Were I happy I'd think it all great fun
Call the Kremlin
Or shoot our streetsigns with my gun
But the masses are screaming out "Art!"
And three times I have seen men die

With too much blood in its veins
the century wilts
Books that were written on pride...
Her lover turns to so much steel in her arms
His heart still beating
"To love and to cherish
till Death."

TO THE STRUGGLE SOUTH

*"Come, lumpen drug fiends, come and
assassinate us in our own land..."*

-Augusto Cesar Sandino
(from <u>El Manifesto Mineral</u>
Jinotega, Nicaragua, 1927)

If a raven sang
I worked till blisters
hardened like clay in desert heat.
If a nightingale cooed
I was hours looking at the rush
of our cabin fire...

We weep for our people
black in the tears of time
or green in the rows of food
till the end.
We say "struggle"
and mean "war"
We say "war"
and mean "let the guarded richones sleep."
I say the edge of a pencil
is sharp.
The shaft of a pen
gun enough for all!

It's the shy side of deafness
turns a cold ear on
our strong right arm.

We are the level
not the rock.
We are the rock
and not the shield.
We are as strong as
each man's choice to be free.
We are as weak as
the pain in every chest.

Then come down from the hills
"Sandinista"
to the sand-in-east-of
the jiggers of revolutionary milk.
Nails across the chalkboards of now.
To what we have fought for is ink
that runs free in your corridor veins.
That cuts through your night like a dream...!

SVAIN

The facts.
I am living in a time when no bird sings.
Dark lamps that light the desks of care.
All looms weaving pain
on the eyes of wide screens
the width of short lives...
A time machine
gleams
    and disappears.
Feather dusters
in the hands of angry clocks.
Five million miles of space---

"If everyone danced
we wouldn't have time for political problems,"

say the ankles that dance
and root deep into fertile ground.

From the dust of shattered bones
grow
the limbs of a new Body;
and I rise like rockets
through neon, to sky!
Somewhere chemicals boil
in huge pots.
Large letters spell

MEDIOCRITY

in a greater sense
like those little white bugs
that bury themselves
in the sand,
I understand---

Not yet   and too late
there are fourteen tribes left
out of the original three,
and none standing.
And I don't hear bells!

In this theatre,
long dirt road of a stage;
the weight of the entire earth

in one small shoulder bag.

THE AGE IS DYING

(The Selected Words of O. Mandelstam)

I.

    Truth is dark.
In oblivion they are singing
the night song;
and how like a beggar the
iron world shivers,
burning
like black ice on one's lips
into hot snow,
melted, flowing,
like a small boat
drifting on the dry river---

    For me the dry air
is empty without you. All
my own blood is gone.
Happiness rolls on like a gold hoop
someone else is guiding.
Everything's happened
before and will happen again,
for there's no way out
of love   and terror,
and after all these years the snow
still smells of ice---

    For us all that's left
are kisses:
      we'll take streetcar A and then
      streetcar B, you and I, to see
      who dies first;
but never mind if
the candles go out,
for I have studied the science
of goodbyes
and it's the paper   not the news
that will save us.
We were born
  to escort the dead
  as spring drifts away and you
  chase it
      waving your hand like a knife.

II.

Miserable is the man who runs
from a dog.
As the earth moves nearer to
truth and to dread,
the Capital hunches like a wild cat
as though we had buried the sun there
and were afraid of the dark.

I am no wolf by blood, and
only my own kind will kill me.
Maybe this is the beginning
of madness.
Long before I dared to be born,
I was a letter of the alphabet, I was
the book everyone saw in dreams.
I fell over my feet.
I swallowed dead air.
(I was choked with space)
My head was deaf.
I read welfare books.
I wanted something to cover my eyes.

I WAS ALONE

Staring into the eye of the sun---

I think it's the locked doors
that have made me drunk.
And I'm bored. My true work
babbles away,
and quiet labour
silvers the iron plow
      and the poet's voice.
The people need poetry! that will
be their own secret
to keep them awake forever,
like the Judas of nations   unborn...

III.

Something is clenched in my chest.
There's a hush there.
No language.
There's no step up to my door.
Quietly warships are gliding through water.
At the edge of the earth the
plow has turned up night,
yet the world's a mistake:
 the back of an axe---
  In the first days of plowing it's so black
  it looks blue,
  still, how handsome looks the fat slice
  of ground on the plowshare!

IV.

In stuffy rooms, in cabs,
in tents,
THE AGE IS DYING....
an age getting over its first drunk.
Life overcomes life. Something
is always missing:
 the old man laying down to sleep
 in the drift of wheat outside
 the window,
 and the famished peasants
 in their felt shoes
 standing guard at their gates---

Now I lodge in the cabbage patches
of the important.
Better to be stuffed up a sleeve like a fleece cap.
Better to be someone with blood in his ink
than being lost to the sky---
Suddenly, all that binds me to language
tempts me to leave it,
and I've come back to my land.
These are my own tears; dry dust
blowing in the streets
 where I saw the world of power
 through a child's eyes
  in a picture book
  I saw the gypsy girl dance
  in a forest of mica
  where flowers never die.
And on what branch does one find truth?

I raise green to my lips.
Among the crickets, the world
fades into oblivion.
The morgue smells
in the nice part of town;

AND WILL IT GO ON LIKE THIS FOREVER

How I wish I could fly
where no one would see me
or trouble me
    with comparison
    or thirst---
For only the grape-flesh of poetry
ever cooled my tongue!

It's dark.
She has taught me truth.

WITH NO CONSTITUTIONAL RIGHT TO DIE

Beneath the tails of glory's greatcoat
there are bodies made of steam
All the world's wealth
merely banknotes in the mind of a bum

They have hooked art up to electrocardiograms
in Saint Paul of the Shipwreck Methodist Church
Bound up books
with covers of neon and electric fuss

IT'S MADNESS!

And I noticed my blood is turning black
like the stripes on a nation's flag
How the circles under her eyes
have become her eyes
and have given in to handbags and noise

Who are we?
Where do we begin?

Il y a quelque chose immodest ici
My country's ass
no longer red shows white through the breath of steel
My stomach full of banker's paste

This is the jazz of what slavery is
Of what man no longer is to woman
on even terms
Of the hell and high water
of every two-thousand years
a Change!

I take back
all the years of weeping I have done
I take back the blisters on my hoe-ridden hands
I yank the hoses from these arms
into which they are pouring dimes

I AM THE TWENTIETH CENTURY!

And have the right to live or die

II. SIRENS SLEEPING ON THE STOOPS OF ROMANTIC LOVE

"At night the self only desires to steep its clangor
in softness, in woman..."

-Vladimir Mayakovsky

"Where are you, my happiness? Sorrow, gloom, confusion.
In the fields? Or in the pub?
Nothing but illusion..."

-Sergei Esenin

BLASPHEMY

to Woman

I'm trying to win a prize

with every poem.

You are the prize.

I am the poems.

Who wins?

When words, like dry leaves,

only cover old ground---

So I'll let my ink take all the bows.

And for myself,

I'll only take your name in vain!

THE PROSPECT

(to the Teeth Mother; naked at last!)

for Robert Bly

You came at me with a green hell in your eyes.
Your teeth were the glass
that race stood against each day
as it combed its sex-strewn hair.
A velvet scarf hung at your throat
like a nation's flag
weeping in pools of its fatal past.
The closer you came
the more blue I could see in your eyes.
The more blue
the closer you came.
And that is how we met.

Now, it's the circles, love,
that have taken away your teeth.
Smoothed out my frown.
Turned the cotton into lace.
Laying in a bed of dreams
centuries deep
and neatly covered in snow---

Tonight, it's quits.
And the pain in the basement of my soul
will go.
But even as we cut and tear at
each other's weak bouquet,
I grow larger still.
For there is much more gold in the sky
than they've told.
Like the life
at the bottom of this silver pan.

WHAT AIN'T THE TRUTH IS A LIE

"Lies can stand up against much in the
world, but not against art."

-*Alexander Solzhenitsyn*

What part of me is it wants you
even more than my ballet?
The half that's full I think.
Like a pound of unsigned poems
in my name.
Or four great tears full of fear
running like pride down
my face that like luck
must always turn away---

Is money what a pauper
sends in vain to a princess?
Love what a poet
keeps down in the dirt like a pig?

Truth is
only what truth has taken away.
To rattle bones before you
would be like hanging oceans up to dry.
Brass bands in the back
of my brawn.
Like new bombs in the brain
before sleep---

You're alone in a cloud
on the tip of everyone's tongue
and I'm the silence standing
still on every stage.
In the parts of my legs that dance
there is a leap no ink has ever seen.
And I'd give it all to
one good gust of wind.
Or a silver star,
as it walks down an open road
toward home.
Where you live.

THE MASKED MAN

No matter where she walked
she walked on silk
like she might have walked in snow.
Or a rusted rug of pine
like dew on forest floors....

On a swing
or like "gods from the sky"
she swung from glass
to the bar where each night I drank wine.
She was something for sale.
Sign hung on her said
"ne touche pas."
My eyes were fingers
on a pair of useless hands.

New in town
I wore a mask.
Man with no name.
"Masked man," she'd say.
And I'd go.
The fate of the moon
in bed with a helpless sun.
And a rose in the door
of a house where she lived with another man.

What really lies behind this mask?
More blood in the snow?

A crystal star
is changing rooms with
the stones of poetic heart.
Where during darkness there is always
at least a touch of night.
But the daylight hours say:
"Keep a fire in the window."
"Let the sleeping and the dead lay---"

LILY IN THE COMPANY OF A ROSE

"Soon far from the rose and the lily, and fret of the
flames would we be,
Were we only white birds, my beloved, buoyed out
on the foam of the sea!"

-W.B. Yeats

From such great heights
it looked like Pegasus would fly
from the wings that made me dance.
Heaven turned to a snow-bound hell,
and the way you smelled
like honeysuckle refusing to die.

Was it my hand that reached out first,
or yours that was attracted to mine?
Wherever the guilt,
two hands committed the crime.

The truth is this:
I am moved more by the fear of going in
than going out on the other side.
It's easy to leave a wilted rag behind.
But it's the absence makes me weep
these diamond tears.
Nothing more.

So, you'll have your house
and I'll have mine.
Together at last.
A lily
and a work-worn rose.

SIRENS SLEEPING ON THE STOOPS
OF ROMANTIC LOVE

Like a sword that is drawn from the stone
leaves its scar
You are that empty space
at night that I'm filling with sleep

What is history to the hole?

Forests of death
Steps that echo in a Druid church...

Like gray hair
on the head of an angry nun
Or words with certain beats
in a line
A man can never die
of old age
For it's not that sirens sleep
on the stoops of romantic love
There is only time tugging there
like dwarfs pulling at their master's cuffs
Birth and blue locks
Every mother's son
in the fingers of a plastic ditch---

On black wings
she flew like no bird
had ever known the dawn
Tamed tricksters with their own tricks
Blew kisses that
went off like bombs
in the gardens of do or die
And he'll die by the moon
near his own grave
Not a flower to his name
His name
whispered by wind
like a bone slides easy
through the skin
at a break
for the last time
near the edge of an endless dream

HELL HAS NO POWER

Snow-red as the sun sets
behind green hills winter
is dreaming of spring
And I am cutting wood
to stoke this chested-warmth for you

In this poor century
"hell has no power over pagans"
the plow no voice over the engine's roar---
I am bringing up dead fish
even in the holes of my nets
there is something wrong with pain

I am wrest of religion
and the cross
and the Crusades
against plastic and beer---
Lay me in bed with the foul
and the geese
and I'll cackle and coo
like all the women in heat

Night has made a pillow of my life without you
Its eyes reflecting off the blue snow
as if the new world meant "love"
or the future mentioned "home"

But I'm wise to silver stars
and the memory of glitter on green trees
And so I sit before a fire
as the early morning sky
inoculates the red wind
And all my ancient thoughts return
like trains of you
on wheels of golden fleece.

HER SEA

Where I am now
there is fire in rock
Sea stroking the hair
of its favorite man
Any bird
in a mirror of blue sky

Because there is wind
in the way I see you
I can breathe no hate
You can sigh no fear

We are helpless to the silver sun
going down between your thighs

Pacific
Peace
A golden road into night
Shadows of Incan past
Blue eyes
calling on the dawn...

CLANDESTINY

Through the hole for a key
in a large bronze door
I looked twice
with eyes of gold
Banging
with the fists of rock---

WHO SAYS SILENCE OPENS DOORS?

And if you utter the word "die"
one more time
I'll scream!
Or pull "No" from the earth
by its roots!

Whatever you want

Your hands down deep in a purse
I'll put diamonds in milk
A flower in each ear
Or a thousand names
for every day you live

Don't tell me that you're dead!
It's the truth that I've
found in the rain
while you were gone...

So, here, take it!
Paint it all on your face
till you look like
a house with big ears
And streets with a broken nose
For there are no vedas in a vacuum
No prize for peace
in a piece of rag---

Listen!

There is a great heat under the earth

WIND IN A GALLEON'S SAILS

"Most of what we do in life, even if
we advance other reasons, is done
because of women."

-Hermann Hesse

Let the words flow through me
like wind in a galleon's sails
And I will reach
to the nearest star
pluck a thousand smiles
she will receive as roses
in a miser's bouquet

For us the sun is taboo
We carry our hearts in cloth totebags
strapped to the middle of our lives

THE MUSE IS SINGING

The sky is dry and
there are lies in my moustache

She was clean
yet wanted to live near the floor
Her breasts were full of light
all men alone at night
read their whorey books by
Paris sang
Weeping to the echoes of lamantines

Pendant le Fête Noire
I am going to step out of this body
like wind in the sails of a galleon
She is the Boom in my existence
The anchor in my joy

SOMETIMES A PIECE OF LIGHT

Sometimes a piece of light
is all of you remained.

I felt a strange heat in my chest
as if anger were building a fire.

We have passed the stage of being coy.
And the sun sets on opposite sides
of our same but different lives
into which we are pounding blue nails.

It was everything.

And nothing in the same breath.
What mind is to memory.
What perfection is to pain---

Where were we born?
Does the snow still lay warm
on those places?
Where all that was written
now seems so much straw.
Where we made the vows of children
that touched our toy skin.

We were hiding in the throngs
that milled in the streets of big cities.
We were shooting stars
in a dark night's sky.

We saw love in a carpenter's sheath.
Building our mountains from dreams.

THE MAN YOU HAVE PULLED OUT OF SOUP

Where was the sea
when they wrote all those books about love?
And you
as I took off for the stars
to search out truth
in the shape of your body at night.
You were hidden deep in my veins.
Like memory in a bomb
ready to go off in another life.
I should be tending the roses
in your windowbox,
washing my hate in your thighs---

We have shifted the blame to a lie.
Lived through what we thought
love itself was,
and were wrong.
The sea heaves,
feeling no guilt for our fear.

Do you know how it feels
swimming through space with no eyes?
Walking blind in forests
of hissing geese?
It's more like hocus-pocus
than dried ink.
Yet you've died five times
before my heart could count two.
And still I won't believe!

What is the man in this dream?
Is he something you have pulled out of soup?
Where are the wings
you said you would bring me to fly?
You're there.
And I'm still here,
on the roof of what I imagine
to be true.
And it is
What I saw in a dream
Came
And went

Before I could kiss you goodbye.

CONSTANTINOPLE

for Philip Lamantia

And it was stars
from where she got the light.
Shining in the brightest eyes
where I was reflected
and knew she had a special touch
where she kept secrets like silent myths
in a wooden box.

From out of knots
in my chest grew a kind of fire.
A fire keeping all that was lonely warm
in a century cold of machines.
Where I envisioned clipper ships
and carriages
drawn by horses of daylight and dawn.
Where she was princess
in every one that passed.

And it was strange.
Like roses received from the unknown.
The clear rock she wore
to her waist in a cross,
clearer than the light she held to truth
that told on everything a lie.

And it was night.
Over tarot and red wine.
Over the whole land
the tide was coming in
over a black-rubied beach,
where my mind ran away
in a unicorn surf
with my body washed ashore

in memory and blue grace....

THAT WHICH IS REAL
THAT WHICH IS TRUE

"I cannot love a friend whose love is words."

-Sophocles

The beginning was "bliss."
Nothing came between us.
Not even time. Not even space.
We kept the same hours.
We ate the same foods....

IT MUST HAVE BEEN THE TRUTH

Other things began to catch her eye.
She found excuses for her beauty.
Compensation for her age.
She hid in books and silence.
And in the bodies of her children.

Her love each night
was brought to me in blocks of dry ice.
Soon we lived alone in the same rooms.
Soon we lived alone.
We met at theatres and cafés.
Or by mistake in the park.

Our old home seemed empty.
I passed by on the city bus.
Heavy bolts guarded her inside.
She loved me. There were other men.

She loved us all.
We had nothing.

THE TEST

In her mind she has tested god.
I could see it in her eyes,
like rusted rings around the moon—
If art were for hire
we'd all be dressed in business suits
and carry a deadly weapon on each hip.
I wouldn't call this a conspiracy,
just something weird that's happening
in all our beds on boring nights.

She knows three things that excite her.
I wipe the love from typewriter keys.

Franz Liszt.
Sex in back seats of chevrolets.
The sea.

III.   THE LANGUAGE OF KNIVES

"Alas, whither shall I climb now with my longing?
I look from every mountain for fatherlands and
motherlands. But nowhere have I found a home; I
am unsettled in every city and I depart from
every gate. The men of the present, to whom my
heart once drew me, are strange to me and a mockery;
and I have been driven from fatherlands and motherlands."

-Friedrich Nietzsche

from "Of Immaculate Perception;"
Thus Spoke Zarathustra

I don't write poems.

I write little miracles.

Sly little miracles--
The kind that scare off mountains

or steady seas.

The kind you are looking for

and are going to find in me.

POETRY

for Bob Kaufman

Where the corners of the world divide
she sits in sponge
Beasts the size of dreams
appear and melt in an orange fog

In the river between
sleep and walking the streets
poetry paddles its dark canoe
A hula dance
on a breast the shape of Mt. Ranier
A sun of forest-green
and white

But it's gone!
Like an August snow
saved from boredom
for the memory of a rainy day...

If something sings
there is a god
If something growls
I will know she's not alone

PETITION TO THE SUN

When there's no hope
there's no use.
There are a million old men
beating illusion with their canes.
And a million wives
in bed with an ape.

What's the point in rain
when you're already wet?
Another fix?

Ah, but the snow this season's dead.
Sheep herded into flats and mirror-drawers
like our ancient pets.
And Diane is a name painted
on the side of trucks
in red.

When you say there is more to making love
than to fuck,
do you mean our astrology's the same?
But you dare not say.
There are too many spies without sex.
And a price on your head
larger than the sum of light
in those starry ageless eyes.

We are a kind of heat
that has known no warmth.
A kind of ice
that melts with our every need.
Come out sun!
My skin lies virgin to your pain!

POEM TO DA VINCI BATHING

In whose eyes are perfect trees
the perception of
some unknown elves
that only know grace by the wind
through the memory of a woman's hair?

And these silent walls
that beat my body back into pulp
that tie me down to the cross
of a mother nature's lie
I defy you!
I won't call your bluff
a poem---

What voodoo magic do your Banks
call death?
And what plastic parts alive?
That wander like gothic streams of spring
through empty rooms that wait.

Red is the number one.
And nine is the light from the sky.
So I won't wait for destiny to call.
I'll ride the stallion home
before dusk
to the barn of my second youth
to dine with the kings and queens of taste.
Where dawn sits
sewing patches on her rags.
And an old man
drawing water for his final bath.

THE LANGUAGE OF KNIVES

If there were ever moon
enough for all that lived
blood would harbour wings
in the air they are cleaning with trees

In a half-finished Hell
blood is frozen on electric lines
where I am going to step
out of this body
turn
and look back:

What I will see will surprise me
That which I miss, will disappear

It's been the prophets of brooms
ranking art to the standards of work
Religion
like language in the beak of a shy bird---

In the dustbins of the planet earth
there is a song singing rain
There are five green trees
And a bowl
In the bowl there is a stone of white light
It comes from the river
And the river comes from dreams

What if future were the last few moments to conceive
And time were scattered bones

WHAT THEN?

In hills beyond the price of pain
Boyhood is chasing a bra
against a stiff wind
Leopards dancing
to the broken jazz beats of a suffix dawn
A gun doing push-ups
to the counts of a rusted cross
And a virgin's silver bell
ringing in the eyes of wind!

MEMORY

*"Memory is not what we remember, but that which remembers us.
Memory is a present that never stops passing. It waits in
hiding and suddenly grabs us with hands of smoke that never
loosen their grip. It slips into our blood: he who is planted
in us and throws us out."*

-Octavio Paz

It was white
before the blue
put its graying head to rest
on a pillow of sleepless stars
And the unicorn danced
while the mares sang sex
from their locked and empty barns---

The moon was a coin
I carried in pockets of old pants
When it came up
gray went down
and she was glass
taken from shattered seas
or broken dreams

In morning
you are there like the dew
around a rich woman's neck
The gypsies are spinning their love
onto spools
as a husky kid throws rocks at the trees...
In the windows at night there is fire
in the frosted panes of recent years
And like a quivering bird I am whistling
the easy tune of youth
on a hollow reed

In worn-out shoes we ran
through age and
being young
Down dark roads
where the doves coo
like crows near the colour red

The ancient elms are laughing
and shaking memory from their hair
near streams that flow through the wheat
to homes that are not really there

EXPECTATION

(after the painting by Richard Oelze)

for Ken Wainio

Magic is seeing what is.

We'll call it a play.
"The chief characters were cities,
and chief events, the streets."
High overhead I flew
on the wingspan of death.
Like a large bird
looking for lunch in the night.

We were lined up in rows on the banks.
Being baptized in our own spit.

No, it was nothing to the rain.

All drains ran to the same sea.
Where rivers would meet near the rocks
throwing dice at the full moon.

She howled like the wolf she was.
Sister to the colour black.
Where Spain slept in bullrushes
and the sun approved.
"Time," she said,
and the rivers opened doors.
One at a time.
All of us went in.

It was one large room
where machineguns danced with clocks.
Wizards asleep on beds of wire
in states of red
and green.

Her eyes mumbled
as she reached for the latch on the door
to go...

To the faithful there comes faith.
To the truthful: truth.

To the worthy there come dreams.

LA MAGIQUE DU BONHEUR

Frame and face to the wall
I have been victim of young crimes
with an expensive heart
seen the omega green
the cold
the cuts of
a silence that brings on sleep

BEWARE OLD PAINS!

In those dreams
of spiritual
and not material gold:
You knew A as God
left me with C
of blue calligraphy
and a diet of brown rice

So come and lift me up old maid!
I'm here giving birth
to the turds that mend your wicked ways
Where we walked the tunnel of red light
through the glom and the layered
fat
the fanatic cream
the merde
and the zoot
    de la langue...
It was the scrubbrush of life
the mustard-kiss of death
knowing
no light without shadow
and no thing whole
without disease

I am here
where the red
and green rocks
    make the black sand
Where I am my own
bête noir
Where light is the only shore
for a tired canoe

under a tonsillectomy of stars!

I WATCH RATS

to Jack Spicer

As I watch rats
crawl in
and out from under the floorboards:
a brown cat.

Nowhere is there such silence.
Not even soft fur
moves from the breeze through windows at dusk
blowing the thin lace curtains---
Cat and mouse.
Warplanes and sheep.

Bits of cheese.
A rat bites into Rimbaud's foot.
No pain.
No sign of blood;
only a large pool in the dirt
where the pipes leaked:
Colours.
Numbers.
Sounds.

I saw nothing of the meal.
Not satisfied.
Only a dark flash
of paws and teeth
that cut through night
like a rainbow with a point...

Upstairs kitchen.
Behind the stove,
ripples in a small milk-filled dish.
Someone throwing stones.
Nothing drunk.
A brown cat.

THE ASSOCIATION

In that dream
I rode bareback   a white stallion.
Learned telepathic the names of all the famous trees.
Sleep was a mattock deep
in southern soil.
And snow   was blue.

I saw faces of ten mythical gods.
Proved gravity to be no more
than a state of mind.
And wrote one great poem each year.

In that dream
I dove off tall buildings.
Never mentioned the word "vain."
And carried guns to arm the sea.

In the distance a calliope sang.
Small children ran in the streets with hoops.
Dumptrucks
hauling city to the land...
.

In that dream
my right wing broke
and I fell
onto the Nimbus of the New World.
The words learned as part of a language
cracked off at the ends
like icicles turning to spring.
And the sun   was green.

In that dream
the perfect woman and the perfect man
sat locked in a cage
behind the bars and eyes of lust.
The Cherokee nation rose up like a human yeast.
Branches of all trees
turned to flutes played by october wind.
And I turned toward the mirror.

Nothing. Changes.

SIERRA BLOOD

for Gary Snyder

Through branches of yellow pine the first star
shines back like a diamond
in the navel of a dark-haired whore.
She is mistress to the sky
as I fish my mind for mermaids
with rubied and silver scales.

It is high in the mountains
and I am spying on spring.
How it stocks its nest of youth
with sacs of raw tears---
We have been defeated by age
in our towns.
And tremble like old toads
on the banks of dried-up ponds.

If you ask me who I am
I'd answer: "Time."
Then bury my head in the dirt
like a root.
I WANT NEW WORDS!
to talk to these trees.
I want new hands
to mend their clear-cut bones!

Over life's loudspeaker
are coming orders of monotonous dreams.
The city ship sinks
into a vinegar sea.
They've chosen me a captain
that sings alone
like a baker without his spoon.
And with anger my teeth are red
cooking the fourth dimension over cold coals
where future stands in its circle and shakes

in a kitchen of death
and disease.

WHAT THE LAND SINGS

for Peter Blue Cloud

Down river
we paddled our dark canoe.
And for whom
do the drums beat?
Loud
to the lives
of those who sit around fires
deep in night's woods---
We sing loud
our songs
to scare fear
we have wrought from wrong deeds.
We know there is something watching.
Its eyes are red.
They gleam through the pitch.

The Hupa chief
tells his eldest son
she is right for him.
The village women knew,
out in the fields picking berries
for the feast.
She would tame his need for war.

We move fast
through the shallow stream.
At the end of this night
there will be nothing waiting
with open arms
but another day.
We have left everything behind
except our past
to look for new gold.

Night grins
as we near the falls.
The drums sing.

DROUTH

When the watershed's dry
there is nothing.
Nothing that grows.
Nothing that shows its head
'bove ground before freeze---

Words are what nations do
to each other's pride.
As we rolled in the wheat
and the hay
while their buildings burned
to the tune of "never say die."

She said "love"
and it rained.
And from that day
I believed!
Moving always west
like a clock keeping track
of lost time.
Searching each pair of eyes,
like every unturned stone,
for that gold.

Again the universe
is chewing on its tail.
And again the drouth
has circumsized our land.
Cycles
like great wooden wheels of fate rolling
across this tender heart.

THE DIFFERENCE

for Stanislaus Szukalski

"We are not what other people are."
We are tears on the edge of marble
or time
in eyes of the young...

He who says Nature is preceded by Art
is only half right.
Half right means only half a man.
Who will follow such a man?

You and I think to make business
the barter of words.
To change each other's mind
to an idea that fits
like new shoes---

"We are not what other people are."
We are how the dancer loves
the sound of his own feet in the snow.
Or the smell of rain
on tin rooves of a second chance...

I want to know,
if we are not the same,
who then I am.
The ace
or the dreaded queen of spades.
Or an old piece of wood
as it drifts onto beach from the sea.

We are many.
Alone with our needs.
"We are not what other people are."

And only the wise grow young.

THE MUSE

for Philip Daughtry

Night no longer has a sky, only a ceiling, and the fires
kept lit on the beaches by the outcasts and bums is all
the light we know. There is great darkness now in all of
us. There is much more time to think than we need; it's
a problem like sex used to be in our towns, and we're all
victim, we're all lost. Everything moves.
There are stories of vast armies of angry souls, that cross
the great sea to come here and take from us our pride.
They must be fools; we've nothing left but a few moments
each day, and a few sides of beef. We all stay close in
large groups to keep warm.
An old man with a cane said he had seen a ray of light
coming out from deep in a blowhole near large rocks along
the shore. We all ran to the spot and looked in. With
our backs turned, in the distance the old man laughed thumping
his cane against the sand. We now no longer hold any hope.
The rains will come soon. Wash away our fires---
There is a young girl with hair as golden-white as the
colour we remember the sun, who sings to the children and
old ones when they tire and are near sleep. She causes
quiet in the camp; a hush that resembles what we used to know
as love. We all listen. And we all try to sing. She is
the thread that holds us to the land, keeps us from the
syren death of the sea. She walks from fire to fire. The flames
dance to her songs. Sometimes there are smiles that burst
through the furrows of old age.
She is our sun, and the moon by which we gauge our days. Our
calendars are based on her rounds. She is our concept of
time. When she no longer comes, we will die. Will be
swallowed up by the sea, every last one, until all that
remains is the sound of sand as it blows against rock. We
think of this when she is gone. We worry, and have made her
our god. She always returns. The dark ones can no longer
negate her.
And we all try to sing....

IV. THE PERSONIFIED STREET

"…Death without tears, our diligent daughter
and servant, a desperate Love, and a pretty Crime
howling in the mud of the street."

-Arthur Rimbaud

SOMETHING DARK

Maybe once a month the moon
would show up with a grin
And the entire human race
would run out from their caves
And mud huts to get warm
And a glimpse of what they'd done

THE EDGE

They said this would be the edge.
I've spent two days searching
for these cliffs.
But it seems the trees
and dense shrubs   will go on forever
unbroken
by any man's dull knife.
Twenty years ago I talked faster than most
any politician
and thought perhaps   a little less---
Well, they told me, and the map says
I should have come to the edge
where that other world, they said, begins.

I can see now
the wise smile of the old mountainman
when I was young.
That I should have looked longer
at the sea.
Walked farther through those golden hills of rain....

JULIET'S WAIT

for A.V.F.

Dickens is dancing
on stage with a beast
Binoculars
in The Great Hall of Doom
are staring back
where black bow ties
are the only things that see---

Here,
there's not enough hope
to fill a growl
Not enough soup
for a blind man's empty tin

She wanted Juliet to wait!
To wedge love into work
like clay in tired old hands
But there is no water in rock
Just like there is no man
who can farm alone

Why do you think the robin's breast is red
Because there is too much heat?
No, it's because all the world is watching
and all it wants to do
is "cheep."

THE PERSONIFIED STREET

If the truth be known
every mountain is a hill.
Every blade of grass a tree.
Is this confusing size with sex?
Or only something like rain with snow.
Let's pretend there's a meadow in your dream
and we're both trains.
Who will finish first?
Dancer or dove?

Peace is like a parade
through the heart of New York.
Sex is the street.
I am the fifty-second floor of mankind
that covers you in a confetti of lovenotes
falling like martyrs from my eyes...
You are looking up and saying yes with
your thighs wide at the crossroad.

Brass bands passing into the womb.

NOUMENON

Tonight
the cold october air
I remember picking corn
and storing grain in a schoolhouse
beneath red sky
in the middle of this land

Tonight I would rather fall in love
than thinking back to a time
when it were true
and the fall chill
wants me to kiss anything that moves
in the memory of blonde hair---

A red leaf
is what I've tacked to my one-room wall
Like a single drop of blood on the page
makes the poem
And it's closer to home here
than I thought the city could
With red wings
Black veils
And memories of gold!

THE RHYTHMS OF LOSS

Into the ear
sound made its way to the drum.
Motion threw the latch on the heavy door.
Music in a metal box.
All love in a vault with the chains.

THERE IS NO REAL PLEASURE IN PAIN

A quiet waltz amongst the roar of guns.
A stream along the flow of city streets.
He who holds baton
is directing traffic at the intersection of darkness
and light.
The body shrinks to the size of ego and fact.

We have lost the land!
Forgotten all the chords.

THE SCRUBBER

Knees
and elbows raw
I have rubbed with the Rich

I am affected

Infected
with the germ
that seeks to bring life
out of death

      GREAT ART

out of the melting pots
of mediocrity.

And the bourgeois in the large houses weep!

ALLITERNATION

Near the folded grip of night
reason sprang free
from the eyes of its lonely jail

They turned out the dogs of wit
and quick lines
They took out the guns of light
from their glass careers

There were
frozen flowers at the backs of stone walls
Fission in the beaks of red fowl
While the halves of the other side
piled weakness in pyramids to a show of force
And a ghost
as it walks down the dirt road from town

My shoes
in the pockets of your tattered old coat....

IN RED SNOW

You're your own salesman.
And I'm my own mud.

TIME SHAKES!

From the stage
we march in rows of one
towards towns
where we live alone.
And wait.

For when it's all down
and winter
and those mirrors turn to tears,
those tiptoes turn to sleep:
we'll stare.

I'll be wrapped in red snow.

PRETENSE IS NOT WAR

Pretense is not war.
Nor bullets in the eye of Law.
We asked for answers,
and got rhymes
in an age of free verse.

What is a schoolboy
in the eyes of a whore?
A banker at the end
of a hoe?

I KNOW

It's the reason we all scream fire
at the slightest sign of smoke.
The answer to every silent "why."

A dark girl in white lace.
Giraffe in a cornfield.
A show of hands.

THE FINAL OAR

A baby born on a black night, on
a stretching moan of wheat
is what is the duty of death,
the final oar,
on IRONy's blue locks.

She looked good in the bodies of other men
or women in rooms, where
late night
and early morning
she saw just enough day to die.
Like wishes to be free.
Panning for diamonds in snow.
Or people home.

Three wrongs have made this right:

All men hate war.
There is anger and cold blood in the eyes of love.
What we want we can and never have.

THE ANSWER

You ask what it is
that is so alone in my words---
It is this:

It's not the streams or open fields.
Not the silent nations of peace.
Or the will to look
a monster in the eyes
with truth.

It's only love

like a young boy who is marched into Church.
Without a single Friend his age.

OF SHROUD; OF SEA; OF ME.....

Waves wash to shore

like a blanket

covering the shoulders

of a deadman

The sun

is saturned by rainbows

The sand quenches

the thirst

of my tired feet

And I lay here

To live again

Only a piece

    of the smallest of living things

9030